ANGEL OF THE BATTLEFIELD

by

Nellie McCaslin

ANGEL OF THE BATTLEFIELD

Library of Congress Cataloging-in-Publication Data

McCaslin, Nellie.
    Angel of the battlefield / by Nellie McCaslin.
        p.   cm.
    ISBN 0-88734-430-5
    1. Barton, Clara, 1821-1912--Drama.   2. Nurses--United States-
-Drama.   I. Title.
    PS3563.C33745A83   1993
    812'.54--dc20   93-2604
                                                                CIP

ANGEL OF THE BATTLEFIELD

A Dedicated Nurse Gives Her Life
for Her Suffering Countrymen

There is little question that Clara Barton was one of the most remarkable women in the history of our country. Her contribution was so great and her activities so numerous that the problems involved in presenting even a fragment of her life are all those of selection. Both to the field of nursing and to public life, she gave of herself freely and generously. Tiny, frail, powerful, courageous—Clara Barton was in every sense a pioneer.

ANGEL OF THE BATTLEFIELD

THE CHARACTERS

STORYTELLER

MRS. BARTON

MR. BARTON

CLARA BARTON, *aged 11 in Scene One; aged 18 in Scene Two; and a grown-up woman in Scene Three*

SALLY, *an older sister*

DOROTHY, *another older sister*

THE DOCTOR

SUSAN

MARY

FOUR BIG BOYS

OTHER CHILDREN *(any number)*

FIRST VOLUNTEER WOMAN WORKER

SECOND VOLUNTEER WOMAN WORKER

FARMER

MESSENGER FROM THE SANITARY COMMISSION

SCENE ONE: The Barton farmhouse in New England. 1832.

SCENE TWO: A country schoolhouse. 1839.

SCENE THREE: A warehouse in the South during the Civil War.

6

ANGEL OF THE BATTLEFIELD

SCENE ONE

THE PLACE: *The Barton farmhouse in New England.*
THE TIME: *An afternoon in 1832.*

STORYTELLER. When we think of battlefields, we don't usually think of women. Yet one of the most remarkable women in American history spent so many years of her life nursing and helping soldiers that she came to be known as "The Angel of the Battlefield." This woman was Clara Barton — teacher, nurse, patriot, and founder of the American Red Cross.

Clara Barton was born in Oxford, Massachusetts, in 1821. Although she was never trained to be a nurse as girls are today, she had her first chance to serve when she was only eleven years old. It was in the Barton farmhouse in 1832, just after David, Clara's older brother, had been hurt in an accident.

(The STORYTELLER *leaves the stage, and the CURTAINS OPEN on the Barton living room.* MR. BARTON, MRS. BARTON, SALLY, DOROTHY, *and little* CLARA *are waiting anxiously.)*

MRS. BARTON. *(Frantic with worry.)* What can be keeping the doctor in there so long? If only he would come out and tell us that David will live!

MR. BARTON. Hush, dear. We must be patient. He would have come out before this if all were not well.

MRS. BARTON. *(Pacing the floor.)* My poor David! He was so quick and strong. How could he have fallen?

7

MR. BARTON. *(Gently.)* It was an accident, Mother. What happened, nobody knows. David was standing on the ridgepole of the barn—the others were working below. Suddenly, someone saw him slip. They brought him home as quickly as they could. That's all anyone had time to tell me.

SALLY. Was he unconscious, Father?

MR. BARTON. Part of the time.

DOROTHY. Did he fall all the way to the ground?

MRS. BARTON. He could have broken every bone in his body. *(Weeping.)* Oh, why doesn't the doctor come out and tell us how he . . . .

(MRS. BARTON breaks down and cannot finish.)

CLARA. *(Deeply sympathetic.)* Please don't cry, Mother. David's been thrown from the gray colt without getting hurt. And he dives off the highest rocks into the river.

MRS. BARTON. I know, I know. But to climb 'way up there! It was man's work, not a boy's.

MR. BARTON. David *is* a man, Mother. But building a barn is a dangerous business, and David was never one to take the easy job, whether it be our own or our neighbor's.

(The DOCTOR enters from an adjoining room. He looks at the others gravely for a moment before speaking.)

DOCTOR. Mr. Barton. Mrs. Barton . . . .

MRS. BARTON. Yes, Doctor, please tell us at once! Is David—will he be well again?

DOCTOR. Your son is seriously hurt, ma'am. But I believe he will walk.

MRS. BARTON. Thank heaven!

DOCTOR. However, it's too soon to tell how long the recovery may take. He may be an invalid for several months.

MRS. BARTON. Oh, I will take care of him. Sally and Dorothy can keep house. And Stephen will help on the farm.

DOCTOR. (Carefully.) There's one thing more, Mrs. Barton—

MRS. BARTON. (Alarmed.) What is that, Doctor?

DOCTOR. It's about the nursing. Your son wishes only his sister—Clara—to care for him.

MR. BARTON. Clara? Why, she's only eleven.

MRS. BARTON. Clara's a mere child, Doctor. Surely David's mind must have been wandering.

DOCTOR. Not when he asked that, Mrs. Barton. His mind was quite clear.

MR. BARTON. (Considering.) Well, Clara has always meant a great deal to him. She's been at his side ever since she could walk. But to ask her to nurse him back to health—why, she knows nothing about such things, Doctor!

CLARA. (Who has been listening intently.) Please let me look after David, Father. I have nursed and cared for animals here on the farm. I know I can do it.

DOROTHY. Our brother David is a bit strange, Doctor, in some ways. He grows despondent easily. Perhaps, of all the family, Clara does understand him the best.

DOCTOR. (To CLARA.) This will not be an easy chore, Clara. He will not recover like a wounded puppy or calf. It will take a long time, and there will be many new things for you to learn.

CLARA. (Earnestly.) I am ready, Doctor. Just tell me what I must do.

DOCTOR. Well, first of all, go in to see your brother. And tell him that you are to be his nurse.

(CLARA dashes off into the adjoining room.)

DOCTOR. Miss Sally, will you and your sister boil me some

water? And while it is boiling, tear some strips of muslin for poultices.

SALLY.
DOROTHY. } Right away, Doctor.

(They leave the room at once.)

DOCTOR. *(To* MR. *and* MRS. BARTON.*)* This may be a long and difficult illness. Ordinarily, I should not approve of a child of eleven being given so great a responsibility. But, frankly, the boy is not out of danger. And his attitude has as much to do with his recovery as anything else. Clara may well be the force which helps him to fight for his life.

MRS. BARTON. Of course, Doctor. We will do whatever you think best.

DOCTOR. It is agreed, then? *(They nod.)* Clara may have to stay out of school for a time. But she's a bright child — it will probably do her no harm.

CLARA. *(Returning with shining eyes.)* I told David that I am going to take care of him, Father. I will nurse him and read to him nights after supper. *(To the doctor.)* I can read grown-up books.

DOCTOR. *(Smiling at her.)* Then your schooling may not be greatly affected, after all. *(Businesslike again.)* But now that it's settled — the first lesson in nursing. *(He opens his bag.)* Here are some pills. The white ones after each meal. The red ones at night when he can't get to sleep. I will show you how to bandage his head and put the poultice on his wounds.

(He hands her the pills. SALLY *and* DOROTHY *return with the muslin strips.* CLARA *begins to tie a small piece of red ribbon in her hair.)*

Here, now. Your sisters have the first strips of muslin all
ready.

CLARA. I want to learn everything, Doctor.

MRS. BARTON. *(Noticing the ribbon.)* Whatever are you
doing, Clara? This is no time to dress up!

CLARA. It's my red hair ribbon, Mother. I just thought it
would cheer David up.

DOCTOR. *(Approvingly.)* That's the first step. And I can count
on you, no matter how long it takes?

CLARA. No matter how long.

(The CURTAINS CLOSE, and the STORYTELLER *comes
forward.)*

STORYTELLER. It took much longer than even the doctor sus-
pected before David was well again. For two years, little
Clara waited on him and nursed him back to health. She
not only stayed home from school, but she scarcely ever
left his side. By the time David finally recovered, Clara
Barton had learned nursing skills which she was to use
again many years later. In the meantime, however, Clara
planned to teach school, and our next scene shows her as
a teacher on her first day at the district school.

SCENE TWO

THE PLACE: *A country schoolhouse.*

THE TIME: *A morning in 1839.*

*(CLARA, now a competent and attractive young woman,
stands on the platform of the empty classroom facing a
number of benches or desks and chairs. She is arranging*

some flowers in a vase, and her books and Bible are on her desk. After a moment, Two LITTLE GIRLS *enter.)*

SUSAN. Good morning, Miss Barton. I'm Susan Boggs. And this is my sister, Mary.

CLARA. Good morning, Susan. *(Shakes her hand.)* Good morning, Mary. Which classes will you be in?

SUSAN. I'm in the fifth grade, Miss Barton. I can read with the sixth, but I'm not very good in arithmetic.

CLARA. Let me tell you a secret, Susan. I'm not very good at it myself. I even have to work hard to keep track of the money in my purse. *(To* MARY.*)* And have you been to this school before, Mary?

MARY. Yes, ma'am. Last year.

CLARA. You look more than seven years old.

MARY. I'm eight. But we live so far away, I didn't come till last year.

(SEVERAL OTHER CHILDREN now come in—both boys and girls. They politely introduce themselves to CLARA, *who shakes hands as she greets them.)*

CLARA. Now, will you all come in and sit down?

(They do so, seating themselves here and there about the room.)

I'll assign your regular places when everyone's here.

(Suddenly, there is a great commotion with scuffling and shouting outside. All hear it, and the CHILDREN *look at each other knowingly.)*

Mercy! Whatever is that?

SUSAN. *(After a moment.)* It sounds like the big boys, Miss Barton.

CLARA. They surely know better than to come into the schoolyard like that.

SUSAN. They know better, but that don't make any difference to them.

CLARA. "Doesn't," Susan. "Doesn't make any difference."

SUSAN. Well, it *don't*. That's why the last teacher left.

CLARA. Oh, I can't believe that.

SUSAN. *(Very sure of herself.)* It was so! And I heard them say they were going to drive out the new teacher before she could shake her fist.

(There is another rough burst of noise from Off Stage.)

CLARA. We shall see about that. *(To herself.)* Then perhaps this noise is all for my benefit.

(FOUR OVERGROWN BOYS stamp noisily into the room. They look CLARA over critically, astonished at her youth and size.)

Come in, boys.

FIRST BOY. *(Rudely.)* You the new teacher?

CLARA. I am.

SECOND BOY. You ever teach school before?

CLARA. *(Ignoring the question.)* Come in and sit down. We can talk later.

(The BOYS do not budge as they stand looking her over. After a moment, CLARA speaks more firmly.)

You are late. For every minute that you dawdle now, you will stay ten minutes after school. Is that clear?

THIRD BOY. *(Insolently.)* It's clear enough.

FOURTH BOY. You know the teacher we had last year?

CLARA. Be seated, please.

(As the Boys *make no move to obey, the* Other Chil- dren *sit with their hands clasped, waiting to see the outcome of the struggle.)*

Clara. I have already asked you to take your seats.

First Boy. We don't know which ones they are.

Second Boy. Yeah! How can we take 'em when we don't know which ones they are?

Third Boy. Anyway, somebody's got the seat I had last year.

*(*Clara *is plainly desperate, not yet knowing how she can gain control of a situation which is obviously grow- ing worse.)*

Clara. Take any seat but take it quickly. We shall begin the day by reading *The Sermon on the Mount.*

(The Boys *reluctantly slide into the remaining seats as* Clara *picks up the Bible from her desk.)*

You all know it, so will you repeat the verses after me?

(She reads aloud, and the Children *recite the verses after her in unison. When she is finished, she replaces the Bible on the desk. Suddenly, one of the big* Boys *shoots a paper wad at* Mary. *It hits her on the head.)*

Mary. Ouch!

Clara. What is it, Mary?

Mary. Somebody hit me — on my head.

Clara. Did someone in this room do it?

Mary. It was one of the big boys, ma'am. Just like last year.

(Suddenly, a ball is thrown from the front of the room to the back.)

Clara. Give me the ball, please.

(The ball is thrown back up front. To everyone's astonishment, Clara *intercepts it.)*

Thank you very much.

FIRST BOY. *(Whistles.)* She caught it!

SECOND BOY. *(Unbelieving.)* Do you play ball, ma'am?

CLARA. Ever since I was a little girl. I had two older brothers; and in order to play with them, I had to learn how to pitch and catch.

THIRD BOY. Let's see you pitch one, ma'am?

CLARA. Very well.

(She pitches him an excellent ball.)

FOURTH BOY. Say! You're all right, Miss Barton!

(Without realizing what is happening and the effect it will have, CLARA and the FOUR BIG BOYS engage in a swift game of "catch." The hostility has suddenly vanished, and a real admiration for the teacher takes its place.)

CLARA. *(Finally putting the ball down on her desk.)* There. That's enough for one time. If you like, we can play a real game out-of-doors after lunch.

FIRST BOY. You bet, Miss Barton!

THE OTHERS. We'll be there!

CLARA. *(Now sure of herself.)* And now, we can begin the day's lessons.

(The CURTAINS CLOSE quickly on a very attentive group of pupils and the smiling teacher).

STORYTELLER. For many years, Clara Barton taught school. She would probably have gone on teaching had it not been for an illness which caused her to take a job in the nation's capital for a change. While she was there, the Civil War broke out. Suddenly, the opportunity to care for the sick and wounded soldiers came to her. Within a short time, she found herself not only nursing but performing all kinds of services for those who needed help. She devoted herself to this cause as she had cared for her invalid brother so many years before.

The third and final scene of our play takes place in a warehouse in the South during the Civil War.

SCENE THREE

THE PLACE: *A warehouse in the South.*
THE TIME: *During the Civil War.*

(The CURTAINS OPEN on a warehouse somewhere in the South. Apparently a place where army supplies are stored, boxes, barrels, and heaps of old clothes are everywhere. CLARA BARTON *and* TWO VOLUNTEER WOMEN WORKERS *are moving busily among them. After a moment,* CLARA *speaks.)*

CLARA. *(Checking off supplies.)* Bandages, medicines, drugs —all over here.
FIRST WOMAN. And the clothing, Miss Barton? All this has come in since last week. What shall we do with it?
CLARA. Leave it here—for civilians. Not only the soldiers are the victims of this war. I've often thought we should be organized to help everyone—women and children as well as the men. But there are so many of them—and so few of us.
SECOND WOMAN. *(Checking another box.)* This must be the food from New England.
CLARA. Oh, yes. Will you read what it says?

SECOND WOMAN. (*Reading the labels.*) "Coffee, jelly, preserves, crackers, soup—"

CLARA. Three carloads! (*Desperately.*) And only one sauce pan to cook with!

FIRST WOMAN. (*Reading from another label.*) "Candles, paper, pens—"

CLARA. So many have given, and they have remembered everything that I asked. The letters to be written, the missing to be found, the spirits to be lifted.

FIRST WOMAN. (*Stopping her work.*) Is it true, Miss Barton, that you have actually baked pies for homesick boys?

CLARA. It is true. And puddings and custards when I had the makings. But not very often, I'm afraid. Most of the time, it's a matter of just getting supplies where they're needed. (*Sighs.*) And the need is so desperate these days.

SECOND WOMAN. I don't see how you've done it all by yourself.

FIRST WOMAN. This warehouse—and the others! The nursing, the meals—

CLARA. But I haven't done it alone. There have been so many who were willing to help. It's getting that help to the front. Ah, that's the difficult part!

(A FARMER *enters the warehouse and approaches* CLARA BARTON.)

FARMER. Is this where I can find Miss Barton, ma'am?

CLARA. Yes, sir. What can I do for you?

FARMER. You're Clara Barton?

CLARA. Yes, sir.

FARMER. Why, you don't look no more than eighteen!

CLARA. Thank you, sir, but I was eighteen a good many years ago. What do you want?

FARMER. Please, ma'am, there's a poor lad strayed onto my place. He don't seem to know who he is—or what regiment he was with.

CLARA. Is he wounded?

FARMER. He's got a bad foot. I don't know if there's anything else. But he needs someone to talk to. Someone to find out where he belongs. He's a soldier, I guess, but he ain't nothin' but a boy.

CLARA. *(Efficiently collecting her supplies.)* I'll come right away. Are you far from here?

FARMER. Five mile—more or less.

(A MESSENGER from the SANITARY COMMISSION enters.)

MESSENGER. Supplies ready, Miss Barton?

CLARA. All ready. My volunteers will show you which boxes they are. I have to go see a poor lad. But when I get back—

FIRST WOMAN. But, Miss Barton! Must you go now? You haven't rested for days!

CLARA. There's plenty of time in the future for that. When the army can rest, I will, too. Now, where's my red shawl?

SECOND WOMAN. Here it is, Miss Barton.

CLARA. Thank you. I'll be back as soon as I can.

(She and the FARMER go out. She is carrying her little bag of supplies.)

FIRST WOMAN. Funny thing how she always likes a touch of red.

SECOND WOMAN. She doesn't care anything about clothes, though. Always wears black. But, you know, I don't think I've ever seen her without a red scarf or ribbon. Like a bright spot of hope in the dark.

MESSENGER. They've got a name for her out there.

FIRST WOMAN. What is it?

MESSENGER. You mean you haven't heard? *(The* WOMEN *shake their heads.)* It's "Angel of the Battlefield."

SECOND WOMAN. *(Softly.)* "Angel of the Battlefield." They couldn't say a truer thing.

(The CURTAINS CLOSE slowly, and the STORYTELLER *returns.)*

STORYTELLER. Yes, "Angel of the Battlefield" was what they called her. And that name stuck for the rest of her life.

When the Civil War was over, Clara Barton finally went to Europe to get that rest she'd promised herself. But there, instead, she found more work to do. The Franco-Prussian War had broken out; and in no time, she found herself again on the front lines, nursing and handling supplies.

It was there that she first heard of the International Red Cross, an organization which helps those in distress just as she had helped them at home. From that day on, she was determined to establish the Red Cross in the United States, where it should serve not only in war but in peace. You see, Clara Barton cared most about getting relief for the people who needed it, whether they were victims of battle, cyclone, earthquake, or flood. It took many years, but in time her dream came to pass. And today, whenever disaster strikes, her Red Cross is equipped and ready to serve.

We have had many brave and courageous women in our land; but no one, perhaps, deserves a higher place than Clara Barton, the woman who gave her life to the needs of her fellow men.

(END OF THE PLAY)

PRODUCTION NOTES

CHARACTERS:

10 women, 8 men, extras, storyteller

COSTUMES:

Pre-Civil War clothing. The women wear tight bodices, full skirts, shawls, and aprons. Their hair is arranged simply, and the colors are dark. The men wear long trousers and frock coats with waistcoats.

SETTINGS:

Scene One: A farmhouse living room. Table, chairs, 2 doors

Scene Two: A schoolroom with a teacher's desk at the front and benches or desks and chairs in rows

Scene Three: A bare warehouse filled with boxes, bundles, bags, barrels, and piles of used clothing

PROPERTIES:

Strips of white cloth, doctor's bag, books, flowers, Bible, ball, papers, pens